DATE DUE APR 0 3

4/5/5			
11/20/22			
GAYLORD			PRINTED IN U.S.A.

THE BEDOUIN

OF THE MIDDLE EAST

ELIZABETH LOSLEBEN

**First American edition published in 2003
by Lerner Publications Company**

Published by arrangement with Times Editions
Copyright © 2003 by Times Media Private Limited

Lerner Publications Company
A division of Lerner Publishing Group
241 First Avenue North
Minneapolis, MN 55401 U.S.A.
Website address: www.lernerbooks.com

Series originated and designed by
Times Editions
An imprint of Times Media Private Limited
A member of the Times Publishing Group
1 New Industrial Road, Singapore 536196
Website address: www.timesone.com.sg/te

Series editors: Margaret J. Goldstein, Daphne Rodrigues
Series designers: Tuck Loong, Jailani Basari
Series picture researcher: Susan Jane Manuel

Library of Congress Cataloging-in-Publication Data
Losleben, Elizabeth.
The Bedouin of the Middle East / by Elizabeth Losleben.
p. cm. — (First peoples)
Includes bibliographical references and index.
ISBN 0-8225-0663-7 (lib. bdg. : alk. paper)
1. Bedouins—History—Juvenile literature. 2. Bedouins—Social
life and customs—Juvenile literature. 3. Arab countries—Social
life and customs—Juvenile literature. I. Title. II. Series.
DS36.9.B4 L68 2003
956'.0049272—dc21   2002001846

Printed in Malaysia
Bound in the United States of America

1 2 3 4 5 6—0S—08 07 06 05 04 03

CONTENTS

WHO ARE THE BEDOUIN?

The Bedouin are an ancient Arab people. They live mainly in the Arabian and Syrian deserts, the Sinai Peninsula of Egypt, and the Sahara Desert of North Africa. There are Bedouin communities in many countries, including Egypt, Syria, Israel, Jordan, Saudi Arabia, Yemen, and Iraq in the Middle East and Morocco, Sudan, Algeria, Tunisia, and Libya in North Africa. Altogether, the Bedouin population numbers about 4 million. The Bedouin share their lands with other cultural and religious groups. Like many people in the Middle East and North Africa, the Bedouin are Arabs—they speak the Arabic language and practice the Islamic religion.

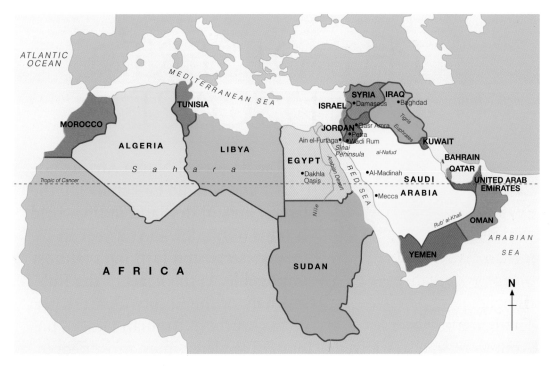

Desert Dwellers

The name Bedouin comes from the Arabic *badawi*, which means "desert dweller." The Bedouin are traditionally nomads. They live in tents and move from place to place in the desert, looking for food and water for their herds of camels, sheep, and goats. The Bedouin are very proud of their culture and traditions. They have preserved their way of life for thousands of years. In the late 1300s, an Arab historian named Ibn Khaldun called the Bedouin the strongest of all the people he met during his travels in the Middle East and North Africa. The Bedouin had the skills to survive in the desert and were very loyal to one another. These traits made their communities tight-knit and helped them keep their traditions alive. Present-day Bedouin nomads still have strong tribal ties.

BEDOUIN GROUPS

The Bedouin are divided into many different tribes. For example, the Rwala Bedouin live in the al-Nafud, part of the Syrian Desert. The Jebaliya Bedouin live in the Sinai Peninsula. The Sanusi Bedouin live north of the Sahara Desert, and the Jahalin Bedouin live in the Negev Desert in Israel. Each tribe is named after an important ancestor. During tribal celebrations, people come together and tell stories about the adventures of their ancestors. Tribes are divided into smaller groups called clans. Each clan is made up of several families that live together in a camp.

THE DESERT LANDSCAPE

Above: Folds in desert rocks contain clues to the land's past.

The deserts of North Africa and the Middle East make up the largest area of dry land in the world. It rains only a few days a year in these deserts, and farming is almost impossible. In the heart of the Rub' al-Khali, or the Empty Quarter, part of the southern Arabian Desert, no living thing can stay alive for long. In ancient times, most people settled near rivers, such as the Nile in Egypt and the Tigris and Euphrates in Iraq. But the Bedouin preferred to live in the open desert.

Below: Desert winds whip the dry sand into spectacular dunes.

More Than Sand

Rocks in the Sinai and northern Sahara can tell us about the history of these deserts. Scientists have found fossils of prehistoric sea creatures in the rocks. This evidence suggests that the deserts were once under the sea. Over millions of years, the sea dried up. The fossils of sea creatures remained preserved under layers of rock and sand.

Canyons

After the sea dried up, forests and fertile grasslands covered the land. But then the climate changed. It started to rain less and less. The rivers slowly dried up, and the forests and grasslands became deserts. River valleys turned into dry canyons called wadis.

Above: Some rocks in the Sinai have been painted blue by an artist.

Floods in Dry Weather

The desert is dry almost all year long. Rain finally falls in spring, in heavy storms that flood the wadis with rushing water. The floods can uproot trees and large rocks and make travel dangerous. Temperatures in the desert change from season to season. Winter temperatures average around 61 degrees Fahrenheit (16 degrees Celsius). But summer temperatures can rise as high as 129 degrees Fahrenheit (54 degrees Celsius).

FIFTY DAYS OF SANDSTORMS

In winter and spring, dry winds blow from the south in the desert, creating swirling sandstorms. The sandstorms blow for about fifty days, so the stormy season is called *khamseen*, or "fifty." The winds have different names, such as *samum* and *harmattan*, depending on which way they blow. They blow as fast as 90 miles (150 kilometers) an hour and can uproot tents and even knock down trees.

PRECIOUS WATER

Above: Oasis springs are a constant source of water in the desert.

Water is very precious in the desert because there is so little of it. The Arabian and Sahara deserts receive only a few inches of rain a year. Bedouin life revolves around searching for water for the family and animals to drink. Carrying water from a source to camp takes a lot of time and hard work. In the last two decades, the weather has been getting hotter and drier in Bedouin territory, making it even harder to find water.

Below: Hard to imagine, but waterfalls do flow in the desert.

Mountain Pools

The Bedouin look for water in many different places. The best source is a *nagat*, or "dripping place," found deep in the mountains. Mountain pools form when rain or dew drips down rocks and cliffs and collects in small shady crevices. Passing Bedouin can enjoy the cool water in the rocky shade, together with birds and other animals that come to the nagat to drink and rest.

Water under the Ground

Desert rain may also trickle down into the ground and fill up underground spaces. Water found in pools beneath the sand is called *shirri'a*. Bedouin find the hidden pools by digging under the sand. In some places, freshwater may be found deeper underground. Bedouin dig wells to reach these deep pockets of water.

Above: The Bedouin store water in animal skins.

Oasis Springs

Oases are fertile places in the desert. They contain freshwater springs, called *'ayn*, that never run dry. Dates, figs, and other desert fruits grow here. Traveling Bedouin often stop at oases to rest by the cool water.

LAND OF THE ROMANS

The ancient Romans once ruled the Mediterranean coast of Africa and the Middle East. Roman soldiers wrote their names on rocks and built wells to collect water. Bedouin nomads still use old Roman wells at the Dakhla Oasis in Egypt and in Wadi Rum in Jordan. Old Roman inscriptions can still be seen in Palmyra near the edge of the Syrian Desert and at the Ain el-Furtaga in the eastern Sinai.

PLANTS IN THE DESERT

Although water is scarce in the desert, many plants manage to survive there. Tough shrubs grow in deep cracks on mountain slopes and on rocky plains. Large bushes grow in sandy areas. When it rains, grass grows up through the sand. Wadis have the richest plant life, including bushes, shrubs, and trees such as the yellow-flowered acacia. After spring rains, wadis fill with the vibrant colors of purple iris, red bladder dock, and other flowers. Bedouin use many desert plants to make food, medicine, and tools.

Above: The iris thrives in the dry climate of the Middle East.

Below: The desert blooms in spring. Birds and bees help to pollinate the flowers of many plants.

Plants for Food

Many desert plants, including figs, bladder dock leaves, and capers, make delicious foods. Date palms grow in oases throughout the year. Dates are very sweet and highly nutritious. They can be eaten straight from the tree or used to make pastries and other foods. Bedouin use date juice to add flavor to bread. Roasted date seeds make a tasty snack.

Above: Fresh figs are lined on the inside with hundreds of tiny seeds.

Medicinal Plants

The Bedouin also use desert plants to cure common illnesses and to keep healthy. Certain roots, herbs, and flowers help relieve rashes, headaches, and stomachaches. Dried sage leaves can be made into a relaxing tea. The Bedouin also burn sage leaves to repel snakes, scorpions, and other dangerous creatures. The forget-me-not, a kind of flower, is boiled in water and used as a mouthwash to heal sore gums.

Other Useful Plants

Bedouin nomads live far from stores, so they cannot easily buy the things they need. Instead, they use plants to make useful items. They hollow out the thick branches of the yassar tree to make storage containers. They use the bark of the acacia tree to make dye for clothing, and they use the acacia tree's branches to make sturdy tent poles. Jebaliya Bedouin carve eating utensils from acacia wood. The Bedouin also stack bushes together to shield their tents from strong winds and the cold night air.

JEWELS OF THE DESERT

The date palm is a very valuable plant. Every part of the tree can be used. The trunk provides wood for building houses and fences. The fruit stalks can be burned as fuel. The leaves can be made into sandals, baskets, and rope. Of course, the fruit of the date palm (*right*) is great to eat. Saudi Arabia has more than a million date palms. In the city of Al-Madinah, date palms line the streets and avenues. Morocco, Algeria, Libya, Egypt, and Iraq are also big date producers. The dates are exported to countries around the world.

DESERT WILDLIFE

Many animals thrive in the desert, even though food and water are hard to find. The Bedouin respect animals. They do not kill animals unless they need food. Some Bedouin work as rangers in the Saint Catherine Protectorate, a nature preserve in the Sinai. The Bedouin can help protect the animals there, since they know the area very well.

Above: The color of the Egyptian gold scorpion blends perfectly with the desert sands.

Dangers in the Sand

Poisonous insects and reptiles lie beneath the silent desert sands. These animals can camouflage, or disguise, themselves. But the Bedouin know how to recognize them and can usually avoid being bitten. Sand vipers often hide near Bedouin camps or under dry firewood. Their bites can kill people. Traditional Bedouin healers treat snakebites, spider bites, and scorpion stings by reciting prayers and breathing or spitting over the wounds.

Flocks in the Sky

Millions of birds fly over the deserts of the Middle East on their way south to Africa for the winter and north again to Europe for the summer. In recent years, many birds have become endangered. Tourists, farmers, and hunters have disturbed nests, destroyed breeding grounds, and killed many birds. But other people are trying to protect endangered birds. They have created parks and preserves, tracked birds to learn more about their habits, and set up breeding programs to increase bird populations. Many Bedouin are involved in these protection efforts.

Left: The fish eagle perches in high places to spot fish in the Red Sea.

Other Desert Animals

Many small animals live in Bedouin territory. The ibex, a wild goat, lives high in the mountains. It is known for running fast over cliff tops. The oryx is a graceful antelope with long thin horns. It stands about 40 inches (1 meter) tall, with a black coat and white bands on its legs. Gazelles live on the plains and lower mountain slopes. The Bedouin sometimes tame them to keep as pets. Wolves, geckos, hedgehogs, and hares also live in the desert. Leopards, hyenas, and foxes are becoming endangered species, as people destroy their natural habitats.

Below: Gazelles have long, ringed horns that curve slightly and taper at the top.

ARABIAN HORSES

For more than a thousand years, Arabian horses have been a symbol of wealth, strength, and courage for the Bedouin. In the past, the Bedouin rode horses when raiding foreign traders and enemy tribes. Horses could run very fast, so they were useful for surprising the enemy. Captured Arabian horses were given to sultans and kings as precious gifts.

THE ANCIENT BEDOUIN

Bedouin history dates to ancient times. The ancient Egyptians wrote about encounters with Sinai Bedouin, who raided their caravans and fought with them in a number of battles. Records of these wars date to 3000 B.C. The Egyptians mined turquoise in the western Sinai. They built walls around the mines as a defense against Bedouin attacks. Other ancient groups, such as the Mesopotamians and Phoenicians, probably encountered the Bedouin on trade routes between Egypt and their own cities.

Right: The Abu Simbel temples, carved into solid rock near the Egyptian border with Sudan, were built around 1250 B.C. for the pharaoh Ramesses II. Four large statues of the pharaoh, each 65 feet (20 meters) tall, sit outside the front of the main temple. In the middle is a doorway leading into a huge hall whose walls show scenes of ancient wars.

Left: The early Bedouin kept their independence throughout the Roman era, often fighting rival tribes.

Meeting the Romans

The ancient Romans once ruled much of Europe, including present-day Spain, Portugal, France, Italy, and Greece. They also ruled the northern coast of Africa and present-day Egypt, Israel, Jordan, Syria, and Turkey. By about A.D. 100, the Roman Empire extended far into the deserts of North Africa and the Middle East. Roman soldiers crossing the Syrian and Sinai deserts often came across Bedouin nomads who traveled these areas.

ANCIENT JEWELRY

The jewelry that present-day Bedouin wear (*above*) has ancient origins. From early times, Bedouin used little pieces of gold and silver to make raised patterns on bracelets and necklaces. They twisted pieces of gold and silver wire into cords. They learned these techniques from the Egyptians. They also made jewelry using Phoenician materials, such as colorful glass beads.

A NEW RELIGION

Traditionally, the Bedouin practiced their own religion. They believed in many gods and spirits. In A.D. 622, Muhammad, a man from Mecca, Saudi Arabia, founded a new religion. It was called Islam. Muhammad died in 632. Afterward, his caliphs, or successors, helped spread Islam throughout the Middle East and North Africa. Many Bedouin converted to the new religion, but they still retained some of their ancient beliefs and customs.

The Spread of Islam

The caliphs amassed big armies. From Saudi Arabia, they set out to conquer surrounding regions. By 641, Islamic armies had taken control of Syria, Lebanon, and Iraq. By the 700s, the Islamic Empire had spread to Iran, Turkey, Egypt, and Spain. It began to invade North Africa around 1050. It was a great trading empire. Islamic merchants traded grain, gold, copper, leather goods, textiles, and perfumes with countries near and far.

An Independent People

Islamic rulers sent ministers to govern large towns and cities throughout the empire. But the Bedouin lived far away from these settlements. They were an independent people with their own leaders and laws. They sometimes came in contact with Islamic traders, but they generally maintained independence from Islamic rule.

Above: An Amazigh woman in southern Tunisia. The Amazigh were the original people of North Africa. In the 1000s, Bedouin invaders converted many Amazigh to Islam.

Left: A desert castle at Qasr Amra. Jordan's desert castles served as inns and hunting lodges in the 700s.

GUIDES IN THE DESERT

Traveling through the desert was difficult and dangerous. Paths in the sand were hard to follow, and people sometimes lost their way in fierce sandstorms. Islamic traders depended on the Bedouin (*right*) to help them through the desert. The Bedouin knew a lot about travel routes, tribal territories, and desert life, so they made good guides.

THE OTTOMAN EMPIRE

Around 1300 a group called the Ottomans took over Islamic lands. The Ottomans were based in Turkey. At its peak, the Ottoman Empire included much of the Middle East, North Africa, and southeastern Europe. Ottoman rulers sent governors to cities throughout their territory to collect taxes and enforce the law. They also sent armies to the desert to take control of the land.

Below: In 1565 the Ottoman Turks attacked Malta, an island in the Mediterranean Sea.

Suleiman the Magnificent

The Ottoman Empire reached the height of its power during the reign of Suleiman I, from 1520 to 1566. Under Suleiman, Ottoman armies conquered parts of present-day eastern Europe and North Africa. Ottoman soldiers also tried to conquer the Bedouin, but they never succeeded. The Bedouin banded together to protect their territory and traditions. The Ottoman Turks could not defeat them.

Desert Raiders

The Bedouin patrolled their territory on horseback. When they encountered Ottoman soldiers or traders, they attacked them with swords, demanding goods and money in exchange for safe passage through the desert. The Bedouin had the advantage in these attacks because they knew all the hiding places in the desert. They were used to the harsh environment. Outsiders began to see the Bedouin as wild and warlike. To protect themselves from Bedouin raiders, the Ottoman Turks built fortresses in the desert and placed guards along roads.

Above: Suleiman the Magnificent on his elegant Arabian horse

EUROPEAN EXPLORERS

In the 1800s, many Europeans traveled to North Africa and the Middle East. Jean Louis Burckhardt, a Swiss explorer, wrote about the people of the Middle East and the ancient ruins he found on his journey. Sir Richard Burton (*right*), an English explorer, traveled through Bedouin territory disguised as an Arab. He wrote books about Bedouin culture.

DAWN OF A NEW AGE

During World War I, which began in 1914, the Ottoman Turks joined forces with Germany. The Turks tried to get the Bedouin to fight with them. Instead, the Bedouin united with other Arab groups and joined the nations fighting against Germany.

Above: A Bedouin messenger speeds across the desert on his camel.

The Great Arab Revolt

The Arabs wanted freedom from Ottoman rule. They wanted an independent Arab state in the Middle East, stretching from present-day Syria to Yemen. Their vision was a nation they could call their own, based on Arab culture and religion. With the help of the British, Arab forces rose up against the Ottoman Turks in 1916. This event was called the Great Arab Revolt. Led by the two sons of their leader, Husayn ibn 'Ali, Arab forces took Damascus, Syria, from the Ottoman Turks in 1918. By the time World War I ended in late 1918, the Arabs had control of present-day Jordan and parts of Syria and Saudi Arabia.

New Nations

But the Arabs did not get the unified nation they had fought for in the Great Arab Revolt. Instead, the Western powers divided the Middle East and North Africa into many separate countries, including Syria, Jordan, Israel, Morocco, and Algeria. New national borders split Bedouin clans. New governments tried to get the Bedouin to follow national laws instead of their traditional tribal laws.

Shrinking Lands

In the late twentieth century, Arab nations began to industrialize. Roads, factories, and towns were built on traditional Bedouin lands. As their territory got smaller, many Bedouin found that they could no longer live the way they used to. They began to leave their tribal lands. They moved to towns and cities to look for jobs.

Left: The clock tower in Riyadh, the capital of present-day Saudi Arabia. The kingdom of Saudi Arabia was founded in 1932.

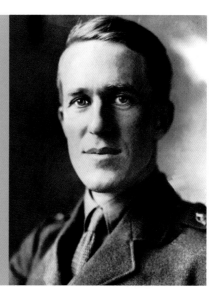

LAWRENCE OF ARABIA

Thomas Edward Lawrence (*right*) was a British archaeologist who traveled in the Middle East in the early 1900s. In 1916, during the Great Arab Revolt, he led a group of Arabs in their fight against the Ottoman Turks. He inspired them with his vision of an Arab nation. Lawrence wrote about this experience in a book called *The Seven Pillars of Wisdom*.

TRADITIONAL BEDOUIN LIFE

Traditional Bedouin life is centered around animals. The Bedouin move to find water and good pastureland for their herds of camels, sheep, and goats. The Bedouin traditionally made, gathered, or traded for everything they needed. They got milk, meat, leather, and fur from the animals they herded. They still get much of what they need from the land and animals. But they sometimes sell animals and crafts for money. They then visit villages to buy things like flour, sugar, and cooking pots.

Above: A Bedouin shepherd watches over his flock.

Below: A Bedouin herds camels using a truck.

Caring for the Herds

Bedouin women take care of the sheep and goats. They sometimes must walk the animals high into the mountains to find water and grass for grazing. The herd might contain hundreds of sheep and goats, and the women must make sure that no animal gets lost or is attacked by a predator. Bedouin men are responsible for the camel herds. Sometimes they have to travel far into the desert to find enough pasture and water for the animals. When they are away from camp, men sleep around a fire under the stars. A boy becomes a man when he is old enough to travel with his father to herd the family's camels.

Moving the Camp

Bedouin traditionally relied on camels to carry their tents and other belongings to new campsites whenever the clan moved. In recent years, many roads have been built through the deserts of the Middle East and North Africa. Many modern Bedouin load their belongings, animals, and even camels onto small trucks and jeeps. They drive wherever they need to go, even deep into the mountains and valleys. Camels have always been a symbol of wealth for the Bedouin. But, in modern times, trucks are a sign of wealth, too.

SHIPS OF THE DESERT

The camel is very useful to Bedouin in the desert. It provides wool, meat, and milk. The Bedouin also use camels for transportation. Because camels can transport heavy loads over long distances, they are often called "ships of the desert." Camels are well suited to life in the desert. They store fat in humps on their backs, so they can go without food or water for days. Special flaps shield their noses from blowing desert sand.

MODERN BEDOUIN LIFE

Many present-day Bedouin have become seminomadic—they stay in one village for a long time before moving on to another place. Other Bedouin have settled permanently in towns and cities. In Jordan, Wadi Rum is home to a big Bedouin community. Tel Sheva is a Bedouin town in Israel. Bedouin who have settled in towns and cities often live far from their tribes. They have had to find new ways to make a living. But they still value their traditions and are eager to teach foreigners about their culture.

Below: Tourists get ready to enjoy a camel ride at Wadi Rum, Jordan.

The Tourist Trade

Tourists from around the world travel to the Middle East to learn about ancient cultures and to enjoy the beauty of the desert. In Jordan, Petra and Wadi Rum are popular tourist attractions. Petra is an ancient city carved from rock. Wadi Rum is a moonlike stretch of desert with sandstone mountains. Some Bedouin who live near these sites take tourists on desert safaris. Tourists can ride camels or jeeps through the sand and sleep under Bedouin tents at night. Other Bedouin work at hotels and restaurants in tourist areas. They send some of the money they earn to their families in the desert. Unfortunately, due to war and economic problems, the number of tourists in the Middle East has fallen in the last two decades.

Becoming Farmers

With the development of towns and cities, the Bedouin are not always able to roam freely with their animals. Some families have turned to farming as a new way to make a living. They have settled in villages, where they tend small gardens of potatoes, tomatoes, and cucumbers. If the farmers have extra vegetables, they sell them in the village market.

GOING TO SCHOOL

Some Bedouin children attend school (*below*) near their camps in the desert. But most schools are located in towns and cities, far from Bedouin camps. For many Bedouin children, going to school involves leaving their families. When children leave home to attend school, it becomes difficult for them to maintain their values and traditions. Bedouin families sometimes move their camps close to town, so their children can attend school without giving up the traditional Bedouin lifestyle.

HOUSES OF HAIR

Bedouin traditionally live in tents made of camel or goat hair. Called *beit shahaar*, or "houses of hair," these tents are well-suited for the nomadic lifestyle. The tents can be easily put up, taken down, and moved from one place to another. They protect people from the hot sun and strong wind. But Bedouin in towns and cities do not move as often as their ancestors did. They live in modern, permanent homes.

Making a Tent

Making a Bedouin tent is a long process. Men carefully cut and dry tree branches to make tent poles. The poles stand 3 to 5 feet (1 to 1.5 meters) tall and are spaced 10 to 13 feet (3 to 4 meters) apart. Women weave cloth for the tent cover, using camel or goat hair. The tent cover is usually 12 to 15 feet (3.7 to 4.6 meters) wide. Its length depends on the size of the family. Women raise the tent cover over the poles and tie it in place using rope. The door is made from a thick leather flap.

Above: A Bedouin lines the ground beneath his tent with colorful carpets.

Below: The Bedouin tent protects the family from the scorching sun and dusty wind.

Inside the Tent

Each Bedouin tent is home to one family, including children, parents, and grand-parents. Inside the tent, colorful carpets woven from camel or goat hair cover the sand. Another carpet hangs inside the middle of the tent, creating two rooms for sleeping: one for the men and one for the women. Larger families make bigger tents with more rooms. The tent of the sheikh, the tribal leader, has four or five rooms, allowing him to welcome visitors.

SEPARATE SPACES

Bedouin women (*above*) and men do not often mix socially. Women prepare family meals in an area behind the tent. Men meet and talk in an area in front of the tent. Strangers can visit only the men's area. Only close female friends and relatives may enter the women's area. But within the family, male and female relatives are allowed to talk freely.

THE BEDOUIN FAMILY

Most Bedouin have large families, often with as many as twelve children. It takes a lot of work to find water, tend animals, and make life in the desert comfortable for every member of the family. Everyone has work to do. Chores depend on age and whether the person is a boy or girl, man or woman.

A Full House

The Bedouin cherish children and usually have very large families. Having more children means there are more people to help with the household chores. Nomadic Bedouin children have many responsibilities, such as taking care of the family's animals and collecting water from natural pools in leather bags.

The Homemaker

Bedouin women are responsible for managing the household. They are in charge of collecting firewood, preparing meals for the family, weaving cloth to make tents, making crafts, and taking care of the children. They make most of the decisions regarding daily events and family life.

Above: Bedouin men go to the market to buy goods for their families.

The Head of the Family

The Bedouin father is the authority figure in the family. He is responsible for making sure that his children and other relatives are safe and well provided for. The father travels into the desert to herd the camels. He sometimes goes to nearby villages to buy items that the family cannot make itself. In camp, Bedouin fathers meet with the sheikh and other men to make decisions on important matters, such as when and where to move camp.

Left: Bedouin women spend a lot of time with their children.

FREEDOM FOR WOMEN

According to Islam, women must be protected by their husbands. Many Islamic women cannot hold jobs outside the home. They can travel only when escorted by their husbands or male relatives. But nomadic Bedouin women enjoy more freedom than many other Islamic women. They can move around camp without a male chaperone. They do most of their work outdoors, often traveling with herds of camels or sheep high into the mountains (*above*).

TRIBES AND CLANS

Each Bedouin tribe is divided into smaller groups called clans. Each clan contains several families that live together in a camp. Most clans have around eight families, but some have as many as thirty.

Below: Bedouin men meet to discuss clan matters.

Family Ties

Blood ties are very important in Bedouin society. Every family in the clan helps every other family. When there are problems to solve, clans meet together as a tribe to decide what to do. When a Bedouin man and woman marry, their families and clans are united. Strong relationships between families and clans help people endure times of need, hardship, and danger.

The Head of the Tribe

Each tribe has a leader called a sheikh. Some sheikhs are elected by tribal members. Other sheikhs inherit the job from their fathers. The sheikh makes important decisions for his own tribe and communicates with other sheikhs. If there is a dispute between two tribes, both sheikhs meet together to decide what to do. The sheikh is responsible for making sure his people are safe and well cared for. He is respected for his leadership, courage, and generosity.

Above: Women in a Bedouin clan collect firewood and do other work in groups. Working together helps strengthen ties between families.

FAMOUS HOSPITALITY

The Bedouin are famous for their warmth and hospitality. Travelers are always welcome in Bedouin camps. Visitors are invited to stay for several days and to eat and talk around the campfire until late at night. The Bedouin believe that welcoming a visitor is like welcoming God. They are known throughout the Middle East for their loyalty and friendliness.

STAGES OF LIFE

Bedouin society is divided into three different age groups: children, married adults, and the elderly. Each age group has different duties and privileges within the family and clan. For example, grandparents and older relatives are respected for their experience, wisdom, and knowledge. They are well taken care of by younger people.

Below: A Bedouin child plays with his family's lambs.

Childhood

Like all children, Bedouin children love to play. The desert gives them a lot of space to run around and explore. They draw in the sand and play games with stones. In one Bedouin game, players have to find a stone hidden under one of twelve cups. Young children have lots of time to play. But around age ten, girls must help their mothers with household chores, while boys join their fathers in herding camels in the desert. Older children also help their mothers take care of their younger brothers and sisters.

Marriage

Young Bedouin women are considered adults when they get married. Everyone in the camp looks forward to a wedding as a way to unite families and clans. After the wedding, the wife moves to her husband's camp to start her own family with him. But she will often visit her parents in her childhood camp.

Left: Old age is a time to teach others about tribal traditions.

Old Age

The Bedouin respect their elders for their wisdom and knowledge. Elderly Bedouin understand their tribe's traditions and history. They pass their knowledge on to younger generations. Younger Bedouin trust in their elders' wisdom and experience. They look to them for help and advice in handling problems. As people get older, it is their children's responsibility to take care of them.

GUARDIANS OF HISTORY

Bedouin elders are the guardians of the tribe's history. They pass down tribal lore and traditions by singing songs and telling stories to younger Bedouin around the fire. The Bedouin especially love stories about the history of their families and clans. These stories unite clan members and help them remember their culture and heritage. Storytelling is also an enjoyable way for younger Bedouin to learn about their culture.

THE BEDOUIN DIET

Dates, bread, milk, and meat form the basis of the Bedouin diet. Coffee is a favorite drink. Traditional foods hold special significance in Bedouin culture, even for Bedouin who live in towns and cities.

Left: A group of Bedouin share a meal from a single platter placed on a carpet in the middle of the tent.

Mealtime

Bedouin women prepare the family meals, but men and women eat separately. Meals are served on a large platter in the middle of the tent. Diners sit around the platter. No one uses plates or silverware. They scoop up food with small pieces of flat bread, using the fingers of the right hand. Each person eats from the section of the dish that is closest. Bread is a very important part of the meal. But Bedouin in the desert do not use ovens. They bake bread on hot metal plates or in the sand under hot coals.

Right: A Bedouin woman prepares to fling a flat dough circle onto a hot metal plate. This is the traditional way to make flat bread. The dough will be left over the fire to puff and brown.

A Special Feast

On special occasions, such as the birth of a baby, a wedding, or the arrival of visitors, Bedouin celebrate with a feast. Their favorite dish is *mansef*. It is made from sheep or goat meat stewed with spices and dried yogurt. It is served on a platter full of rice. Bedouin feasts bring together people from different parts of the desert and help strengthen family and tribal ties.

Sweet Desserts

Bedouin women make special desserts for feasts and celebrations. *Halawa* is a sweet candy made from sesame seed paste and honey. Bedouin often eat halawa when traveling in the desert. It reminds them of home. Wild figs and dates are other special desert treats.

COFFEE AND TEA

When a traveler visits, the Bedouin father immediately welcomes the visitor into the shade of the tent and offers sweet, hot mint tea. It is served in a small glass, usually topped with a sprig of fresh mint or sage. The Bedouin also like to drink coffee (*above*) with family, friends, and visitors. Coffee is brewed with special herbs and a spice called cardamom in a tall copper pot over a fire.

BEDOUIN FASHION

Traditional Bedouin clothing provides good protection in the harsh desert environment. Women make clothing for themselves and their family members by hand. They may weave cloth from camel or goat hair or buy it from village markets. Traditionally, Bedouin wore handmade leather sandals. But they now often buy sandals at the market.

Above: This man wears the full Bedouin attire, complete with a dagger in his belt.

Traditional Clothing

Bedouin men wear loose white robes in summer. During winter, they wrap themselves in long woolen cloaks to keep warm. Bedouin women wear simple loose dresses that cover their arms and legs, both as a sign of modesty and to protect their skin from the hot desert sun. For decoration, women embroider colorful geometric designs onto the sleeves, seams, and hems of their dresses.

Right: Bedouin women spin, weave, and sew. First, sheep fleece or camel or goat hair is spun into yarn. The yarn is then dyed—red, blue, green, orange, or some other color. The colored yarn is hung in the sun to dry before being woven into fabric to make rugs, bags, clothes, and other items.

Jewelry for Women

Bedouin women wear lots of jewelry. They wear special necklaces for protection and good luck. Each necklace is a metal chain hung with coins and bells. Many coins date from the Middle Ages or even Roman times. Women also pierce their ears and wear large earrings made of silver or gold. Before a Bedouin woman gets married, her husband-to-be gives her beautiful jewelry as a sign of his promise to take care of her.

Bedouin Headgear

Both men and women wear special headgear as protection from the hot desert sun. Men wear a *kafiyyah*, a long cloth headdress kept in place by a black headband. A married woman traditionally wears a veil over her hair, a sign of modesty and family honor in the Islamic religion. She also wears a *burqa*, a veil that covers her face below the eyes. The burqa is decorated with coins and shells.

Above: This Bedouin woman wears a head-dress and veil decorated with colorful embroidery and beads and strings of coins and shells.

BRAIDED HAIR

Bedouin women are slightly less conservative than other Islamic women. Many Bedouin women do not cover their hair completely. They wear thick braids bordering their foreheads and let them show from beneath their veils. Girls start to braid their hair at age fourteen or fifteen. The braids show that the girl is ready for marriage.

BEDOUIN CRAFTS

Many Bedouin nomads sell handmade crafts at weekly village markets. On market days, the women leave camp for the village. They arrange their crafts on large pieces of cloth on the ground in the market area. The women talk with one another, while tourists and shoppers examine the crafts. At the same time, the women teach others about their culture. They sometimes invite passersby to sit and drink mint tea, while they explain their way of life and the importance of their traditional crafts.

Camel Saddles

Every Bedouin man owns a camel saddle, made of carved wood with a leather seat. Women weave wool blankets that cover the saddles and make them more comfortable. The Bedouin often sell used camel saddles to tourists as souvenirs.

Right: Bedouin display their crafts along the road during a festival in Jordan.

Woven Carpets

Above: A handwoven Bedouin carpet with geometric patterns

Thick carpets, called kilim, cover the ground inside Bedouin tents. The carpets help keep sand out of the tent and make sleeping and sitting more comfortable. Bedouin women weave the carpets from camel and goat hair. They color the yarn with natural dyes made from plants and flowers. Kilim come in different sizes. Each one has a different design of colorful stripes and shapes.

Support for Bedouin Crafts

Bedouin Crafts of South Sinai is an organization that helps Bedouin in Egypt. The women make embroidered crafts that show the region's flora and fauna. The crafts include kilim, sheepskin saddlebags, and shawls decorated with colorful sequins, beads, and pompoms. These crafts are sold to visitors at the Saint Catherine Protectorate.

BOTTLES OF SAND

Many Bedouin sell small bottles of colored sand (*above*) as tourist souvenirs. Bedouin artists dye the sand many different colors and pour it into bottles in a special way. They write the names of people and places and even draw pictures of camels and mountains with the different colors of sand.

39

THE BEDOUIN LANGUAGE

The Bedouin speak Arabic, the main language of the Middle East and North Africa. Arabic is spoken mostly in the back of the throat and has many deep sounds. The Arabic alphabet has twenty-eight letters. It is written from right to left. Some English words have their roots in the Arabic language. For example, our words *sofa*, *caravan,* and *algebra* are derived from Arabic. Our numbers zero to nine come from the Arabic numeral system. The Arabic language has many dialects, or variations. The Bedouin dialect is very poetic, with many sweet and polite expressions.

Above: Arabic script. There are eighteen letter shapes. Dots added to the shapes result in a total of twenty-eight letters.

Bedouin Sayings

Many Bedouin sayings express cultural and religious beliefs. One greeting is "Assalamu Alaikum," which means "Peace be with you." Bedouin welcome visitors by saying "Ahlan wa Sahlan," or "Rest as in your home." If asked how they are, Bedouin answer "Alhamdulillah," or "Thanks be to God." And when Bedouin talk about something that might happen in the future, they always add "Insha Allah," or "If God wills."

Arabic Words

The Arabic language has a thousand words to describe horses, including the parts of a horse, its color and markings, and its movement and speed. Here are some other Arabic words and phrases you might try using: *jamal* (camel), *sahra* (desert), *bint* (girl), *walad* (boy), *om* (mother), *ab* (father), *sabah al-kheer* (good morning), *salaam* (peace), and *shukran* (thank you).

Storytelling

The Bedouin have a rich heritage of folklore and poetry. Many popular stories have been told for hundreds of years, passed down from generation to generation. The stories and poems are not written in books but are stored in people's memories and recited by storytellers. At night families gather around the campfire to listen to stories about the adventures of their ancestors and poems about the beauty of the desert.

Left: A Bedouin reads the Quran, the Islamic holy book. The Quran was first written in Arabic, but it has also been translated into other languages such as English.

MYTHS AND LEGENDS

Bedouin folktales tell of magical creatures (*above*), both evil and good. There are also legends about the Arabian horse. A favorite Bedouin story tells how a merchant's son made his fortune with his magical horse. The young man had an evil stepmother who tried to poison him. But his talking horse warned him against her plots. He left home, disguising himself as a beggar and his magical horse as a donkey. The young man became a servant in the sultan's palace and fell in love with the princess. One day raiders attacked the palace, but the young man and his magical horse overcame them. Afterward, he revealed his true identity and was allowed to marry the princess. Together, they returned to his family and lived happily ever after.

BEDOUIN BELIEFS

Originally, the Bedouin believed in many gods, spirits, and natural forces. Muhammad, the founder of Islam, convinced many Bedouin to give up polytheism, the belief in many gods. After Muhammad's death, most people in the Middle East and North Africa, including most Bedouin, converted to Islam. But the Bedouin did not completely give up their belief in spirits and natural forces. These beliefs still affect their cultural and religious practices.

Right: The magnificent Dome of the Rock mosque in Jerusalem.

Islamic Beliefs

Most Bedouin are Muslims, meaning they follow the religion of Islam. Islam is based on a holy book called the Quran. Muslims fast during the holy month of Ramadan, pray five times a day, and give charity to the poor. Each Muslim is supposed to make a pilgrimage to Mecca, Muhammad's birthplace, at least once in his or her lifetime.

Above: Bedouin bow in prayer.

Traditional Bedouin Beliefs

The Bedouin still retain many of their ancient beliefs. They believe that good and evil spirits live in the world around them. According to Bedouin folklore, some evil spirits take human form and others haunt certain places. Bedouin holy men cleanse people and places of evil spirits by praying over them. The Bedouin also believe in kind spirits that bring good luck and blessings.

RESPECT FOR NATURE

Bedouin in the desert depend on natural forces like water, rain, and good pasture. They believe that everything in the environment is connected, including people, trees, animals, and water. So respect for nature is a central part of Bedouin religious beliefs. The Bedouin believe that when people do not care for the environment, God will send floods or other natural disasters. According to Bedouin beliefs, nature stays in balance only when people live by the traditional values of Bedouin culture.

A TIME TO CELEBRATE

Celebrations are a special part of Bedouin life. Even the arrival of a visitor is cause for celebration and thanksgiving. Bedouin celebrate Islamic holidays with prayers and feasting. Weddings are also important, talked-about community events. During celebrations, Bedouin always give thanks for God's goodness.

A Traditional Bedouin Wedding

On the day of her wedding, a Bedouin bride wears an elaborate dress, and her friends decorate her hands and feet with an orange dye called henna. The men of her tribe perform the *ardha*, or sword dance. Carrying swords, they dance side by side to the beat of drums, while a poet chants verses. Guests arrive, bringing gifts of sheep or money. At the end of the ceremony, the bride mounts a camel fitted with a special saddle and travels to the groom's camp. A week after the wedding, the bride visits her parents. She brings a sheep and some rice, sugar, and butter to show them that she is living well and has all she needs in her new home.

Right: Musicians add rhythm to a Bedouin wedding ceremony.

A Time to Fast and a Time to Feast

Islamic Bedouin eat and drink nothing from sunrise to sunset during the month of Ramadan, which falls at a different time each year. When the sun sets, people have *iftar*, a small meal of dates, soup, and fruit juice. They stay up late into the night, celebrating with their families. Before sleeping, they eat a larger meal of carefully prepared vegetable dishes, meat, and special desserts. At the end of Ramadan, people celebrate the feast of Eid al-Fitr. Children receive presents, while their parents thank God for the family's many blessings.

MUSICAL INSTRUMENTS

In Bedouin camps, the clan gathers round the campfire at night to listen and clap to the sounds of traditional musical instruments. Bedouin musicians play hand drums, simple reed flutes, and the *mihbaj*. The mihbaj is actually a wooden coffee grinder. When hit with the hands or a stick, it becomes a percussion instrument. Musicians play the *rababah* (*above*) to accompany love songs and poetry. The rababah is a single-stringed fiddle with a bow made from horsehair.

GLOSSARY

ardha (ARD-hah): a sword dance performed at weddings

'ayn (ah-yeen): an oasis spring

beit shahaar (bait shah-ahr): a Bedouin tent made of camel or goat hair

burqa (BUR-kah): a veil worn by a woman that covers her face below her eyes

caliph: an Islamic leader

caravan: a group of people traveling through the desert, usually pilgrims or merchants

clan: a group of Bedouin families from the same tribe living in the same camp

dialect: a variation on a language

fossil: the remains or impression of an ancient plant or animal

Great Arab Revolt: the rising up of the Arabs against the Ottoman Turks in 1916

habitat: the natural home of a plant or animal

kafiyyah (kah-FEE-yah): a headdress worn by Bedouin men

khamseen (kham-seen): the season for sandstorms and the name of the hot wind that blows from the south

kilim: a carpet woven from camel or goat hair

mansef (mahn-sef): a special meal of stewed lamb, spices, and rice

nagat (NAH-gaht): a pool of fresh water found in the desert mountains

nomads: people who move from place to place, without a permanent home

polytheism: the belief in more than one god

predator: an animal that lives by killing and eating other animals

Ramadan: the Islamic fasting month

sahra (SAH-rah): the desert. The name Sahara for the desert in Africa comes from this Arabic word.

sheikh: a leader of a Bedouin tribe

shirri'a (shee-REE-yah): freshwater found in the desert by digging under the sand

tribe: a group of people related to a common ancestor

wadi: a dried-up canyon or riverbed

yassar: a useful desert tree with light green leaves, white bark, and bunches of brown pods

FINDING OUT MORE

Books

Alotaibi, Muhammad. *Bedouin: The Nomads of the Desert*. Hove, East Sussex, England: Wayland, 1986.

Crociani, Paola. *Bedouin of the Sinai*. London: Garnet Publishing, 1994.

Ghazi, Suhaib Hamid. *Ramadan*. New York: Holiday House, 1996.

Husain, Sharukh. *What Do We Know About Islam?* New York: Peter Bedrick Books, 1996.

Johnson-Davies, Denys. *Animal Tales from the Arab World*. Washington, D.C.: AMIDEAST, 1995.

King, John. *Bedouin*. Austin: Raintree Steck-Vaughn, 1993.

Videos

River Jordan: Waters of Life. PBS Home Video, 2000.

Taleb's Lamb. Clearvue/EAV, 1984.

Young Voices from the Arab World: The Lives & Times of Five Teenagers. AMIDEAST, 1999.

Websites

<http://www.pbs.org/empires/islam/>

<http://www.saudiarabia.net/info/culture.htm>

<http://www.website1.com/odyssey/week3/upclose.html>

Organizations

AMIDEAST
1730 Main Street NW, Suite 1100
Washington, D.C. 20036
Tel: (202) 776-9600
E-mail: <inquiries@amideast.org>
Website: <http://www.amideast.org>

Center for Contemporary Arab Studies
241 ICC Georgetown University
Washington, D.C. 20057
Tel: (202) 687-5793
E-mail: ccasinfo@georgetown.edu
Website: <http://www.ccasonline.org/information.htm>

Center for Middle Eastern Studies
Teaching Resource Center
Room 511, 1737 Cambridge Street
Cambridge, MA 02138
Tel: (617) 495-4078
E-mail: <bpetzen@fas.harvard.edu>

INDEX

ABOUT THE AUTHOR

Elizabeth Losleben is a freelance writer based in Cairo, Egypt. She was born in Montana and grew up in Kenya. She studied English and comparative literature at the American University in Cairo. When she is not writing, Elie is busy planning her next trip across the desert. Her works include *Henna: History and Traditions in Zanzibar* and articles on African and Arab culture. Elie loves the freedom and adventure of her life in Egypt, but looks forward to returning to East Africa in the future. She would like to thank Maarten and her sister Tamar for their endless enthusiasm and encouragement.

PICTURE CREDITS

(B=bottom; C=center; I=inset; L=left; M=main; R=right; T=top)

Bes Stock: title, 14–15M, 37T • Camerapix: 8–9M, 32–33M, 40–41M • Camera Press: 8T, 10–11M • Christine Osborne Pictures: 6T, 6–7M, 10T, 11T, 22T, 22–23M, 25I, 26–27M, 29T, 29I, 31R, 39T, 44–45M, 45I • Focus Team Milano: 27T • Getty Images/Hulton Archive: 18–19M, 19I, 21I • HBL Network: 15I, 30–31M • The Hutchison Library: 9T, 20–21M, 27I • Nik Wheeler: 11I • North Wind Pictures: 15T, 17I, 20L • Photobank: 33T • Sonia Halliday Photographs: 34–35M • Tor Eigeland: 4M, 34T, 35I, 43T • Travel Ink: 36L, 36–37M • Trip Photographic Library: cover, 2, 3, 7T, 12T, 12–13M, 13T, 16–17M, 17T, 19R, 24–25M, 28–29M, 38–39M, 39I, 40L, 41I, 42–43M • Yvette Cardozo: 23I